Serving

Kari Gunter-Seymour

To Sue ~
All good things!

SERVING

Cover design by Kari Gunter-Seymour

Crisis Chronicles #97
ISBN: 978-1-940996-48-6
1st edition, 2nd printing

Published 26 March 2018 by
Crisis Chronicles Press
3431 George Avenue
Parma, Ohio 44134 USA

crisischronicles.com
ccpress.blogspot.com
facebook.com/crisischroniclespress

CONTENTS

ACKNOWLEDGMENTS

We gratefully acknowledge the editors of these journals where several of the poems appeared, sometimes in slightly different versions:

Clover, A Literary Rag: PHOTO 1985
Common Threads: Ohio Poetry Association Anthology: DEPLOYMENT DAY
The LA Times, Clover and Still: The Journal: SERVING
Still: The Journal: AFTER THE FARM, THE APARTMENT ON HOPE DRIVE
Stirring: SIX MONTHS INTO YOUR SECOND DEPLOYMENT
Yellow Chair Review: COURAGE
Gyroscope Review: TEN O'CLOCK, THE DAY ALREADY
    THREATENING, THE THING ABOUT YOUR DAD,
    MIDDLE EAST VETERAN'S WIFE
All We Can Hold: A Collection of Poetry on Motherhood, Sage Hill Press:
    NIGHT MOVES
Vine Leaves Literary Journal: SPLINTERED
Red Earth Review: BASEMENT
Rattle: A LETTER TO JANI LARSON ON THE MATTER
    OF SGT. BERGDAHL
Kudzu: A MIDDLE EAST VET'S MOM ATTENDS THE PARADE
Rock & Sling: NO WORD FROM KANDAHAR

To all who serve, have served and to their families.

PHOTO 1985

There you are, cherub-faced, rice cake with peanut butter,
and little Willie Thompson, balancing yourselves up against
that old house in need of paint, your hair curling up
in the noonday heat. I remember those Oshkosh bibs and tiny
red tennis shoes, and how not long after, we made plans
to leave the farm without your father. That summer I grew

pole beans and Roma tomatoes in raised beds
filled with bottom land soil and cow manure,
pushed up the hillsides in a tottering wheelbarrow.
By fall, multicolored jars lined the cellar shelves while
zip-locked zucchini loaves rested in the deep freeze,
awaiting snowy days when we'd huddle together, grateful

for our hand-me-down wood burner. I miss the smell
of lilac from the heirloom bush where you would hide,
and the cooing pair of mourning doves perched on those
electric wires just outside the kitchen window, ever marking
the day we left Meigs County, where marijuana grew thick
behind barns, alongside butterfly weed and gray-headed coneflowers.
Those last afternoons we walked the tracks hand in hand,
making up songs, going nowhere.

DEPLOYMENT DAY

I'm your mama, is why I cried.
Your tactical gear
slung across your back,
spit-polished.
Final boarding call,
undermining our every breath.
Your hand thrown up one last time,
cold fluorescence bouncing
off your newly shaved head.

Retracing steps to the parking lot,
a wilderness of doubt gleamed
in the slant of dust-furred windows,
grimacing summer sun.
I ran back inside, unstrung,
thinking one last hug might make less
painful your walk into expedition.
Like when you were a baby
and there was no reason to hold you,
only I never wanted to put you down.

SERVING

Remember that time your dog died and I didn't tell you for months
because you had deployed and George Bush was shouting,
Bring it on and we were all thinking that Korea was fixing to blow.
But when I emailed to say we were headed for West Virginia,
you fired back, *Mom, where is Annie?* and I had to say she was hit by a car.
I sent brownies loaded with black walnuts from the old home place.

Or when you called me from Iraq asking me to
talk to people about donating shoes and I told you it was hopeless
because of the tsunami, everyone was already donating.
You said *Hell with that* and your unit threw in their paychecks and bought
all those families just outside Fallujah new shoes off the Internet.
I made two hundred popcorn balls wrapped in wax paper.

Or that February you came home for R&R, so sad and sick.
I baked your favorite meatloaf and you said you couldn't possibly,
but I gave you doe-eyes so you ate and threw up all night,
into the next day, saying over and over *Sweet Jesus,*
please, make it stop and I knew you weren't talking about the meatloaf.

Or the day after Sergeant Crabtree went to Vegas and blew
his head off in the hotel bathroom, while here at home your
best friend got arrested for selling narcotics and you said neither one of them
needed to and maybe wouldn't have if you'd been there. So I shipped
molasses cookies thick with Crisco frosting all the way to Kandahar.

Or the afternoon your farm boy fingers tried to clamp the artery
on that precious baby girl, near the valley of Arghandab,
while her father screamed for Allah and blood soaked your uniform
when you hugged her to you as she passed.
I drenched that fruitcake in brandy for three days.

3

But mostly it was the night your daughter was born and we
locked eyes across the birthing room. I thought to myself,
skillet-fried chicken with candied sweet potatoes, fried okra,
lima beans with bacon, cornbread and aunt Margaret's hot fudge cake.
We used the good dishes and grandpa Oris said the blessing.

AFTER THE FARM, THE APARTMENT ON HOPE DRIVE

Just the two of us,

cramped city dwellers,

subsidized and lonely,

listening to the McKinley boys

thumping their Big Wheel

across our ceiling,

their daddy shouting

one of you boys better

fetch me another beer.

Giving me shivers recalling

the streaks of red and purple

mushroomed crosswise on their mama's face.

Always thankful when it grew quiet,

even knowing all the lights were out

and neither of those boys had scrubbed their teeth.

Beside myself, finding you

and Timmy Moreland crouched behind

that Ninja Turtles sandbox cover,

dodging BBs from his brother's Red Rider

which got taken away only after he shot

banzai clean through their Magnavox,

causing his maw-maw to miss her favorite

America's Funniest Home Videos.

That Christmas you played with G.I. Joes

bought from the dollar store, delivered by Santa.

We baked sugar cookies from scratch,

rode the bus downtown to see the lights.

Many a sleepless night, long after
tucking you in, I flipped on the swag light
hanging over the kitchen table,
sat down to notebook and pen,
waiting for the next words to come.
Turns out the danger in the writing,
Son, is that you will remember
all you've worked so hard to erase.

THE THING ABOUT YOUR DAD

I could lay on the guilt.
Say if you hate your dad
you'll end up like him.
Bitch your own Karma.
Not like if you got caught
with a joint or skanked
on someone's girlfriend.
I'm talking about *divine decree*.

I would be the first to admit
heartless disregard is the worst.
Not even a postcard
the whole time you were in Iraq.
Though there was that one summer
he taught you all the words
to *Rubber Soul* and to shave
even before you needed to.

Face it: he's a phenomenal liar.
Off the tracks more than a little,
he said it made him mental,
thinking of ways other people
could fuck up perfectly good lives.

You're wasting years, Son.
Simple math.
A person can't go around
telling people what to do with their lives
as long as he has
without eventually believing
he knows what he's talking about.

COURAGE

It was hot that night, thick, every scent amplified,
wisteria mingling miserably with the compost pile.
I got up to shut the window, flip on the air conditioner,
though you know I'd rather have crickets and coyotes lull me,
out of habit, check for email on my cell beside the bed:

Your Uncle Bob passed over this evening. Doctors poked needles and
tubes, fishing for some thingy we could not pronounce, though a wiry
little nurse was kind enough to show us a chart. Go in, don't go, the
odds were questionable.

You may recall Bob fancied himself quite the gambling man.
He said he was feeling lucky. Remember all those trips to Vegas? In
those days the man could dance, Contra, two-step, West Coast swing.
Drag me all over the county.

He once told me he shot some kid's toe off in Vietnam. Said the kid
was fixing to kill himself, so Bob shot him. Got him sent home. Bob
lost his promotion over that, but never once spoke of regret. He'd be
disappointed if I spoke of any now.

In the stillness, screen gone pale in the dark, I remember clearly,
just before you deployed to Iraq, I gave powerful thought
to shooting off *your* toe. All the while trying to think clearly about
what it would mean to you to leave Army life behind.
Some days I still wish I had. Those times you are trip-wired,
in that space between breaths, where the tang of mortar fire
and fresh blood lingers, and even the top-shelf whiskey
cannot cover the rumble.

I remember Bob saying he believed a person's spirit
could hover up just before that last rattle-riddled breath.
When I called bullshit, he pledged, scout fingers in the air,
my place would be his first stop.
I wish he *was* here, his fancy footwork stopping the night
dropping hard, like a slammed window.

TEN O'CLOCK, THE DAY ALREADY THREATENING

Light making the whole place look queer—
sky dark, angles and shadows
ratcheting everything down.
Tops of the oaks toss back and forth,
clacking their branches together.

Behind them a rumbling.
Thunder? Someone's truck
down-shifting to take the hill,
life somehow slipping out of gear?

I taught you to dream this yard in Ohio
where the grass holds the shapes of your feet,
where clouds are the breaths of trees,
the wind their voices.

Prayed it would ward you,
the blood and bone smell of it
overthrowing the hiss in your head.
They can say anything, do anything,
bring anything out at any moment,
hope to do you in.

You will have spring rain,
the tin roof, the window sill,
the smell of fresh bread,
your rascally black dog
haunched and cock-eyed,
waiting by the mailbox.

SIX MONTHS INTO YOUR SECOND DEPLOYMENT

I wake to flat hair,
the tug of time spidering
across my reflection
tightening over my
forehead's bone.

Beyond the drafty glass
sit yellowed fields
and ruined gardens.
A lone bird pecks
at some once-seeded thing.

I am a brittle leaf
trapped against a wire fence,
a trickle of rusty water
teasing like the sense
of something waiting to unfold,

leaving only the wait.
I conjure *what if*s,
consider omens.
Beg strangers to pray for you,
make absurd promises to God.

NIGHT MOVES

We leave out
through the back gate,
past the old barn,
straightaway into the woods.

I watch as you run
rock paths and deer tracks,
hollows moist and smoky
in the morning sun.

I don't yell at you even once
for not staying on the trails,
sliding down on your backside
and stomping in the creek.

Bits of leaf and pine needle
hitchhike in your hair.
You stop to point out a wildflower
and make up stories

about the way trees shape a forest.
Red squirrels scatter.
We both get wet under the waterfall.
I lift a hand to block the sun

and I am falling weightless,
landing hard, the bedside lamp
reminds me you are a soldier now,
and the battle for Kandahar drags on.

In that space between breaths,

my fingers reach out,

comb leaf bits

from your soft boy hair.

PANNING FOR GOLD

Pack waterproof boots
you said, the streams of Colorado
swollen and chill even in summer.
You seemed glad to see me,
but after a few days of trying
and neither of us finding our way through it,
we hiked up into the bluffs to pan for gold.
Small flecks, nothing to speak of,
but we were proud of them.

Funny which thoughts get said out loud,
like how I feel about the use
of marijuana as a medicinal,
or how much you love your old dog
who is not long for this world.
What it's been like for you, home,
looking after your daughter between
community college and trips to the VA.
Did I ever wonder how things might have been
had we not left the farm to try our luck in the city?

Did I remember that neighbor boy
who was always asking, *Is them your chickens?*
We would rest in the porch swing,
watching the rain, eating saltine crackers,
drinking well water from an old thermos,
a nest of barn swallows to keep us company.
Your soft boy head, earthy and damp,
nestled in the crook of my shoulder.

Seems even then you were trying to tell me,
though I could not hear, so taken was I
by the flash of lightning.

As the sun took its leave,
we headed down the mountain,
tuckered and hungry.
You turned the radio to an oldies station.
We sang along, making up our own words
for the tunes we could not remember.

STAY-AT-HOME DAD

It's the damn meds, Mom.
I hold my tongue,
finish bathing the baby.
I toddler, she says,
just like you taught her.
You apologize.
Not yourself these days.
Night sweats, unspeakable dreams.

If only they would listen,
you say, looping thumbs
in denim pockets, pacing the tile floor.
I help you and your bum arm
wrap the little guppy in a towel.

We talk about
what to make for dinner,
scribble a list for the grocery.
You say maybe
this time you'll ride along.
First time in months.

We wait for you in the driveway,
motor running,
the baby in her booster.
I want to give someone
a talking to—
have a face-to-face
with that supervisor at the VA,
write a letter to Obama.

Outside the sky is bitter
with soot, long winded.
From the back seat
the baby flags her arms,
ready to go.

MIDDLE EAST VETERAN'S WIFE

Sunshine finds you on the sofa,
heat inching forehead to chest,
stillness with a tremble of movement.
Sacred in that landscape,
where sleep knits real and unreal.

They say your mama was a whisperer,
reaching out to stray or wounded.
Not just dogs and cats, but crows,
mice, once a raccoon.
Her eyes, that touch,
silent words from a language
she somehow knew she had—
for wellness or the good death.

Soon he will wake,
stumble from the bedroom.
You will love him even as he screams,
a rapid fire of bitter words, despair
like fever dampening his upper lip,
eyes feral, memories in flashes and arcs,
chaotic, like mongrels
spilling through a torn fence.
He imagines himself as being held
in some kind of pen, waiting
to be released back into his life.

Edging up, you'll breathe his name
like a secret, reach out, give off a glimmer
of something like light, or hope.

SPLINTERED

I could not manage the gloves,
chunk after chunk, fresh-split firewood,
that sliver sliding in unnoticed,
but for a tiny tingle,
in the struggle to keep up.

It was not to be needled or tweezed
besting me from all sides,
my face sphinctered
in concentration, sweat,
setting myself down
on the wedge planked floor.

I day-dream the beach,
your tiny boy legs brown,
sand stamped, face striped with sun.
I choke on clouds, thrown forward,
your assault rifle cocked,
cradled in the crook of your arm.

Shrapnel, pinpricks gray and blue
dot your cheek and brow.
The numb sodality of death
festers, fills your head with cruel grace,
your memories impossibly wide.

BASEMENT

They wait for you there,
down the narrow stairs,
inside the long shadow where lichen grow
gray in wall cracks and silverfish dance
like free men around empty Jack bottles
and the sagging couch:
shadow brothers, commiserating.

You pray out loud
that self-mutilation and starvation
will somehow bring an end to the torment
of your *Jesus Christ make it stop* ritual.

Play: Your body hurling
toward the Bradley's dash, then
snapping back as if rubber bands
were strapped to your backside.
A jackdaw scratches at the cracked
window pane, black as night,
screaming *Move! Move! Move!*
while blind muzzles fix on your skull
and German death metal bands
pang-pang what's left of your hearing.

Rewind: You don't remember
the body bags, only the zippers.
And feathers—a shitload of feathers,
and the taste of fresh blood,
copper, tin, salt.

A LETTER TO JANI LARSON ON THE MATTER OF SGT. BERGDAHL

We love our sons.
Raised them rich on farm land
or city streets, or Hailey, Idaho.
Taught them honor, to step up
for right and good.
Even so, it may prove true
that your son is responsible for six deaths,
though a spokesman for the Pentagon
can't confirm.

As for my son, he stopped counting.
Had to, lest he turn the weapon on himself.
You'd be amazed how clearly
a soldier can see his target
through a military issue scope.
Brown eyes, sometimes blue,
a dark mole beside the nose,
the awful realization defining
each face a split second
after squeezing the trigger.
Hooah!

It's fight or flight.
Some stay, some flee.
Some get rewards,
some come back alone,
hauling body parts of friends
in zippered bags,
while people in the free world

drink their lattes
and complain.

An admiral on TV today said
when one of your shipmates
goes overboard, you go get them.
You don't ask whether he jumped
or was pushed or he fell.
You go get them.
That's all well and good, admiral,
but what are you supposed to do
when the whole damn ship is sinking?

A MIDDLE EAST VET'S MOM ATTENDS THE PARADE

Athens County, Ohio

I had all but decided to skip the Veterans Day parade this year,
that endless train of local beauty queens atop hay wagons,
tone-deaf high school bands, poodles dressed in khaki.

The VFW Harley club rumbles the pavement, American
flag T-shirts under leather fringed vests. Our ears ring
long after they *vroom-vroom* past. The parade marshals,

two World War II vets, shiver in the backseat
of a flag-draped convertible. Color guard and ROTC
march by in formation, flags waving. Children squeal

delight at the vintage fire truck, its long-winded siren,
old-time penny candies thrown by rubber-clad firemen,
and the mascot Dalmatian also in rubber, trotting alongside.

At the Civil War monument, a peach-faced young woman
belts out the Anthem. I look around. *Oh, say, I do see*
that most don't bother to put hand to heart.

I suck in air near the high note, fingers crossed—
she hits it. The mayor speaks highly of those who have served,
shares the names of several veterans he has known personally,

makes note of the two seated next to him, who he just met.
The speech dwells on American pride, predicts a glorious future,
scarcely touching on toll or sacrifice. American

Legion Post 18, clad in green and navy, present arms
and the twenty-one gun salute. Seven times three, *click, click, fire!*
A short blonde veteran, Iraq we are told, lifts her bugle.

The WWII vets wobble to their feet, salute.
Day is done—her eyes closed, profile tilted skyward,
Gone the sun—each note perfectly pitched, sharp, held

an extra second, moaning, breathy, like boys who fall
in battle. I am undone. Stumbling across the grass
I barely notice neighbors. A few embrace me, thank me

for your service. *Thank me? Jesus Christ!* Out of nowhere
some Barbie look-alike says *Y'all come to brunch,*
and I am ashamed of my reaction, which I barely manage

to conceal. Stepping back, I excuse myself, wonder how
there will ever be an end to it, admitting this only to myself
and now you: *Lord have mercy*, I wanted to punch Barbie in the face.

NO WORD FROM KANDAHAR

You begged to go fishing,
cut a hole in the ice.
Please, Mama.
I'll bait the hooks myself.

Come spring
you asked again.
Wrapped a picnic
in an old bandanna.

Trial and error,
life jacket strapped,
you found harbor
in the stillness where
both boy and fish seek prize.

Lord help me.
I would gladly bleed
to have you here tonight
on that rough rock bench,
cane pole in hand,
each breath a puff of frost.